SECRETS TO AN

UNBREAKABLE

SUPPLY CHAIN

A guide to building resiliency

Disclaimers / Legal Information

All rights reserved. No part of this book may be reproduced, stored in a retrieval system, or transmitted in any form or by any means without the prior written permission of the author/publisher, except in the case of brief quotations for the purpose of writing critical articles or reviews.

Notice of Liability

The author and publisher have made every effort to ensure the accuracy of the information herein. However, the information contained in this book is presented without warranty, either express or implied.
In no event shall the author or the publisher be responsible or liable for any loss of profits or other commercial or personal damages, including but not limited to special, incidental, consequential, or any other damages, in connection with or arising out of the furnishing, performance or use of this book.

Trademark Notice

Rather than indicating every occurrence of a trademarked name as such, this book uses the names only in an editorial fashion and to the benefit of the trademark owner with no intention of infringement of the trademark.

Copyright © 2021 Mr. Howard Knapp

accounting advice. All rights reserved, including the right of reproduction in whole or in part in any form. No parts of this book may be reproduced in any form without the written permission of the copyright owner.

Copyright Information

©2021HowardKnapp

<u>About the Author</u>

My name is Howard Knapp.

While serving in responsibilities as a supply leader and Army logistics officer, I have gained experience in multiple supply chain areas.

I understand the importance of on-time delivery along with controlling the cost of purchased materials. I bring a diverse perspective to the table

through the eyes of a veteran, project manager, and complex problem solver.

My background, while extensive, isn't traditional. Accomplishments include Eagle Scout, Auburn University graduate with a supply chain bachelor's degree, and serving as an Army Logistics Captain. I have unique experiences with civilian and military supply chains in both leadership and technical roles.

Throughout my career, I've strategically built my career around Logistics. From the military, as a Company Commander for three years in a Transportation Unit, I oversaw 200+ soldiers and

$255,000,000 worth of equipment, on the civilian side as a Production Supervisor, I managed 11 assembly technicians. For the past 3 years, I have been a buyer in the highly technical and regulated aerospace manufacturing industry producing civilian and military applications.

What you can expect from this epub:

This ebook is a guide for business owners, supply chain professionals, and anyone who wishes to gain the knowledge and expertise to improve resiliency within their supply chain. This includes a step-by-step process that thoroughly analyzes and adjusts any supply chain to make it robust and resistant to disruptions. I have incorporated the best principles and lessons learned from both my military and civilian supply chain experience to help you create your own "unbreakable supply chain."

How to reach me:

Email: howardsknapp@gmail.com

LinkedIn: https://www.linkedin.com/in/howardknappcpsm/

Website: https://hknapp.com/

CONTENTS

INTRODUCTION

With the current political unrest and a world torn by coronavirus, we have experienced unprecedented disruptions in our personal and professional lives. As countries have shut down their borders and economies have slowed, keeping supply chains operating on budget and on time is becoming exponentially more difficult.

I have put together this guide to help you identify which components of your supply base are vulnerable to interruptions and what actions you can take to create a business continuity plan.

Our supply chains are so intertwined that the impacts of global events are felt everywhere. It is now more important than ever that supply chain leaders like you balance resilience and efficiency to improve the reliability of global networks.

Before we dive in, let us discuss the details of a crisis and why it's important to actively manage supply chain risk.

Webster dictionary defines a crisis as, *"An unstable or crucial time or state of affairs in which a decisive change is impending."* From a supply chain perspective, a crisis is an event that causes one or multiple activities to be disrupted, resulting in a complete or partial disturbance of the flow of goods or services. Resiliency on the other hand, is the ability of an organization to **absorb and adapt** in a changing environment. A resilient supply chain will be able to deliver its products in a wide spectrum of market conditions.

The emergence of COVID-19 globally demonstrated the importance of a resilient supply chain, and, if you're like most supply chain professionals, recent events may have caught you completely off guard. From 2020 and throughout 2021, the cost of supplies has increased, caused sporadic demand, expedited freight costs, as well as from paying premiums to buy up supply and hold capacity. In a recent study done by the McKinsey Global Institute, 14% of firms experienced losses from supply chain disruptions that cost over $1 million. In another report published in August 2020, it was sated in the report that more than 60% of global supply chains are designed to maximize cost efficiency rather than resiliency and agility. I highly recommend this site to stay up to date on business and economic topics that can affect your business and your supply chain operations.

I can tell you that by following the principles in this guide, you can have a supply chain that can provide superior service while increasing efficiencies and controlling costs.

Professionals need to take the time to plan for a crisis and review the potential major impacts it will have on your supply chain before it happens. In this guide, I discuss potential issues to look for and how to address inefficiencies in your supply chain that are leaving you vulnerable to risk and most importantly, money lost!

CHAPTER 1:

Supply Chain Analysis

Applying Military Methods for Analyzing Your Risks

A model organization that is efficient at proactively addressing supply chain risk is the United States Army. Serving as an Army logistics officer at both the battalion and brigade levels, I have done my share of analyzing a battle space for potential threats using the exact method I discuss below. Before you can address the tactical risks, first you must take a step back, and look at your supply chain from a strategic view.

Let's define strategic vision as the ability to:

- Visualize the longer term

- Implement a broader view of the organization, seeing it in the context of its competition and the current economy

- Define the path by which the firm can grow in the long term

- Repeatedly move the organization forward in creating greater value

This type of thinking benefits others to understand the vision so that it can be translated into challenging and meaningful goals and connects the big picture to tactics and short-term goals.

In 2021 and beyond, a strong supply chain is not immune or sheltered from disruptions and must be able to quickly react. Analyzing your supply chain strategically is that first step. Knowing the composition of your supply chain and being able to predict the impacts of current and future events accurately is vital to maintaining a healthy supply chain in this highly volatile environment.

Military units follow the acronym PMESII-PT while doing mission analysis which can be used by civilians to better understand a supply chain.

The acronym stands for:

Political

Military

Economic

Social

Infrastructure

Information

Physical Environment

Time

My first exposure to mission analysis was during the Army course for captains, Logistics Captains Career Course. By following the specific categories in PMESII-PT, we knew all angles were considered during our risk assessment of the battlefield. PMESII-PT provided a framework we could use to thoroughly examine the traits and characteristics of a specific area. Whether your supply chain is local or spans multiple countries, you can use this approach to analyze risk from a strategic perspective.

Political	Military	Economic	Social
Attitudes towards your country	Military forces	Economic diversity	Demographic mix
Centers of political power	Government paramilitary forces	Employment status	Social volatility
Type of government	Unarmed combatants	Economic activity	Education level
Government legitimacy	Military functions	Illegal economic activity	Ethnic diversity
Influential political groups	Military Influence	Banking	Religious diversity
Political Party Views	Military legitimacy and corruption	Growth Domestic Product (GDP)	Population movement
			Common languages
			Criminal activity
			Human rights
			Diseases
			Cultural norms and values

Infrastructure	Information	Physical Environment	Time
Construction pattern	Public media	Terrain	Cultural perception of time
Urban zones	Information management	Natural hazards	Measurement of time
Utilities present	Information infrastructure	Climate	Key dates
Services		Weather	Key events
Transportation architecture			Key holidays

Use PMESSI-PT by applying this method to your current supply chain. Choose a supplier or specific category type to analyze following the acronym. Majority of the information you will need will be online, so it would be wise to begin your initial research there. Other sources of information can be from your actual supplier, colleagues, and your company leadership.

Most have never looked at a supply chain from a high-level strategic view and most have not traced their supply chains from beginning to the end customer. It may be surprising just how complicated the modern supply chain is. Find a product that will have the most impact for your efforts and begin there. This could be product in the most valuable line for the company. It could be product with the most associated material cost, or a product line that has seen the largest cost increases in recent years.

Now let's dive deeper into PMESII-PT.

Below is a chart which lists helpful factors for your analysis based on the Army publication TC7-102 (Operational Environment and Army Learning Document) which is available online for your reference:

Political- This portion focuses on the total political power within a given area and reviews the entire political structure, such as administration and state institutions. The factors analyzed include the effectiveness and legitimacy of the current Government and are reflective of current policy issues. Political friction leads to tariffs, new regulations, or policy changes that directly affect supply, pricing, and availability.

A good starting place to analyze how your supply is influenced by political factors is by visiting the US Department of State's Bilateral Relations Fact Sheets; this will provide useful information about the relationship between a country you are analyzing and the United States.

Go here to learn more:

https://www.state.gov/u-s-bilateral-relations-fact-sheets/

Carefully analyze areas with poor political stability since it is most likely to experience supply chain breakdowns. Many professionals overlook how local political conditions influence a supply chain's efficiency, so being familiar with the current political climate is crucial. Other political disruptions include union strikes, port closures, tax policies, trade disputes, tariff wars and even container shortages. These can all have direct impact to the total landed cost of a product and can cause prices to increase. Some accounting systems put freight through a separate ledger account , meaning the full cost of a "Landed" product will never be truly known.

To minimize your exposure to political risk, a company may consider purchasing political risk insurance. Several organizations like AIG, specialize in political risk insurance to mitigate the impact of an adverse event if you choose to pursue business in an unstable geo-political area.

Here are a few recommended political insurance sites:

https://www.aig.com/business/insurance/political-risk

https://www.zurichna.com/insurance/trade/politicalrisk

Nearshoring, which brings manufacturing and business back to the United States, can also be an option.

Military- Especially for global supply chains with international suppliers, analyzing current military events regarding supply chain risk is a prudent idea. Including this factor in your analysis forces you to consider the potential disruptions the military can inflict on your supply chain.

The military in any country has the potential to interrupt supply chain operations. Militaries can confiscate material for their use or impound equipment and vehicles as the military seems fit. Where necessary, military units may directly affect supply chains by disrupting the movement of road networks with detours or road closures. Keep in mind that even specific areas of a country can have more military activity than others, so be sure to analyze impacts at both the local and national levels.

As a commanding officer, my unit was activated numerous times to assist with the Santa Barbara floods, and Southern California wildfires through 2018-2020. The military was called upon to close down roadways and redirect traffic. Be sure to review the current military environment of your supply chain so that you do not get impacted by these types of delays.

Keep in mind that military disruption events may be difficult to predict. Military actions can be quick and decisive with no warning. It is important that the disruption be identified as soon as possible to allow for a quick pivot within your supply chain. If a military disruption is detected, you can quickly shift supplier capacity from your primary to your second supplier to temporarily sustain operations. Having strategic level of inventory to compensate for the disruption would also serve as a buffer until a more permanent solution is obtained.

Economic- Here the analysis encompasses economics of both individual and groups related to producing, distributing, and consuming resources. Factors such as company financial stability, the main form of industry, and income for the area are crucial for this analysis. Conducting business with suppliers who are not financially stable significantly increases your risk. Remember to analyze not only the vendor's financial situation but also the local economic environment. Both can influence supply chain operations.

A great source for analyzing supplier financial risk that I personally use is Dun and Bradstreet's (D & B) supplier risk manager.

 Check it out here:

https://www.dnb.com/products/third-party-risk/dnb-supplier-risk-manager-2-0.html

This resource uses massive data files and analytics to provide predictive scores and ratings on the likelihood that a business will file for bankruptcy, cease operations, or become inactive. This is a trusted source that numerous corporations subscribe to. Using this when initially analyzing your supplier for risk prior to conducting business works best. Anytime a new supplier is selected for new businesses, I always obtain a DnB risk assessment report. This prevents me from starting a partnership that can lead to unwanted financial conflict or headache down the road.

Experian also provides similar supplier risk reports on demand:

https://www.experian.com/small-business/supplier-check-reports

Social- Social focuses on the cultural, religious, and ethnic composition within an area. This focal point encompasses everything from local beliefs to values, customs, and behaviors.

The social analysis is vital for scheduling, communicating, and setting expectations with your vendors, etc...

From a cultural and even business perspective, countries all over the world have both similar and unique holidays that can create unforeseen delays. For example, the Chinese celebrate their New Year on different days each year, which impacts China's production calendar. In 2020, the Chinese New Year fell on January 25. In 2021, the Chinese New Year was on February 12. During this time, China shuts down and manufacturing significantly declines or stops. If you were not anticipating this closure, the pause in your production flow would come as an unwelcomed surprise. Being cognizant of delays like this will allow you to properly forecast and increase order quantities to cover for the lack of deliveries during that time.

It's important to keep in mind that this is not limited to international supply chains. Even the cultures within the different regions of the United States and even from company to company vary. Start by reaching out to your vendors. This simple request can be the difference between being surprised or being prepared.

When researching an area, consider four main social categories that can impact your supply chain:

Material culture: This is understanding the technology used by   most of the populations.

Language: The common language spoken may impact the context of information and business relationships.

Religion: Often a major cultural influencer than can affect aspects of life such as holiday activities and work times, which ultimately impact output.

Ethics and Values: This influences the business relationship. Conducting business with unethical companies can also lead to unwanted negative publicity.

Infrastructure- When it comes to the transportation of your product, the most important piece of your analysis is the infrastructure. Infrastructure represents the elementary facilities, services, and installations that make up the area.

Questions to get you started with this analysis include the following:

What transportation networks exist and are utilizable?

What utilities are present and operational?

What is the capacity and capabilities of the network?

Countries like China have a well-established logistical distribution network which is one of the issues that prevents offshore manufacturing companies from returning to the United States or investing in other cheaper countries. Some countries may have cheaper labor but do not have the infrastructure to support reliable distribution or throughput capabilities that is required of the modern supply chain. Evaluate an area with infrastructure that supports reliable transportation of your products with minimal delay and efficient cost. A way to do this analysis like this on your own is with google maps. Look for desirable features such as nearby ports, train stations, and multiple road options. Undesirable features can include congested road areas and limited road networks.

Information- When reviewing a supplier or your supply chain, ensure a reliable and secured information network is present. Consider how they communicate information formally and informally.

Ask yourself the following questions:

Does the Government protect you from copyright or trademark infringement?

How controlled or open is the information environment?

An effective operating supply chain requires reliable and constant communication to stay synchronized. Without it, operating a supply chain is nearly impossible.

A method of information protection is to use confidentiality agreements between two parties, such as a signed non-disclosure agreement (NDA). An NDA is a legal contract between at least two parties outlining confidential material, knowledge, or information that the parties wish to share. For example, if technical information is traded between your business and your supplier, your supplier will not be able to legally share that information with any other parties including your competitors. However, although an NDA will help you protect your data, the agreement may not be legally enforceable in other countries, so be sure to complete your country-specific research before beginning any legal process.

Visit https://hknapp.com/ for a free copy of a standard mutual Non-Disclosure template

Physical Environment- The physical environment includes evaluating the geography, self-made structures, and identifying local weather characteristics to understand possible natural disasters that could occur in each area. Understanding which natural disasters are predominant in your region is crucial for preparation. Once these are recognized, you will be able to begin anticipating the potential impacts of a disaster and can plan appropriate mitigation efforts.

With the increasing influence of climate change comes a heavier impact on business. By having accurate predictions and adequate preparation time, you can mitigate adverse weather impacts by increasing your on-hand inventory, rerouting / delaying shipments or alerting customers of potential delays. AccuWeather has a new advanced weather forecasting system for businesses that provides accurate weather forecasts and warnings. It allows quicker and more precise information targeted at helping you make informed business decisions related to the weather. Being able to see a natural disaster before it hits can give you the time you need to execute your emergency evacuation and preparation plan (in chapter 5 of this guide, I discuss the emergency plan in greater detail).

Weather report available here:

https://business.accuweather.com/

Time- Time is all inclusive of the timing and duration of activities, events, or conditions. Not every country will perceive time identically so you must determine what the cultural perception of time is for your chosen area. In a global supply chain that spans across multiple nations, each country may have its own unique perception of time and sense of urgency.

In the United States, being punctual and schedule-abiding is a cultural norm that differs from countries such as the Philippines or Greece. In these states, there is a looser understanding of timeliness and adherence to a schedule is less of a cultural priority.

As you complete this full analysis, keep in mind that no specific variable by itself should prevent you from conducting business with a supplier.

However, by holistically observing ALL the variables from a tactical and strategic view, you will see your supply chain in its totality.

If you see multiple shortfalls in PMESII-PT analysis, you may have identified an elevated risk in your supply chain. Still, you should conduct supplier searches or create an emergency plan for each category. In the military, having unfavorable PMESSII-PT variables can scrap entire plans. With multiple shortcomings, we would need a complete reevaluation of actions taken which can result in mission cancellation and/or more planning sessions. This is why, thoroughness is of the utmost importance.

CHAPTER 2:

Supplier Risk Examination

When analyzing whether your supply chain can withstand a crisis, it needs to be examined from not both a strategic perspective, and from an operational level.

Look for locations of your supply sources, routes, distribution points, inventory levels, and manpower.

One way to do this is through a supplier risk analysis. This approach is used to assesses a supplier's capabilities and weaknesses.

The provided charts have a few examples of core factors that directly impact a supply chain's resilience:

Abilities	Description	Examples
Current and Potential capacity	Capacity is an indicator of a supplier's potential to produce or provide service during crisis situations. In military logistical units, capacity is considered when assigning missions. In both the civilian and military world, having an ideal balance of utilized and reserve capacity is important. Ideal capacity is 80-85% with 20-25% of that capacity set aside for reserve.	Reserve Capacity, labor capacity, Back up
Sourcing	The ability to quickly and efficiently change the quantity and type of outputs. Sourcing in the simplest form, is the ability to acquire resources. With the dramatic change in consumer demand, sourcing has become an art. The organization that can find the resources needed quickest, has the best chance to adapt.	Contract flexibility, Expediting, alternate suppliers
Manufacturing and Operational Flexibility	The capability to quickly and efficiently change the quantity and type of production. The ability to adapt and adjust operations in order to maintain continuity of supply is critical. In the military, an enemy attack causing vehicle damage can instantly reduce capacity, while a snowstorm on the east coast can instantly reduce customer demand.	Scalability, Re-configurability, changeover speed, multiple pathways and skills
Visibility of Operations	Situational awareness on the status of working assets and the environment. Ensure that your suppliers can track operations. With the growing complexity of supply chains, there is an increased need for tracking a higher number of products through the supply chain. We have entered an age where tracking our packages can be done at our fingertips and consumers have more control than ever on. Apple has released ID tags to even track letters.	Information technology, Status reporting, external monitoring, Key performance indicators

Weaknesses	Description	Examples
Financial strength	Ensuring an organization is healthy and likely to survive economic disruptions. Analyzing financial risk will assist with the risk of failing, an increased understanding of how the firm is managed, and ensure long term existence of the supplier. In the military, an enemy with more financial resources will likely be a more formidable competitor.	Cash reserves, Insurance, Profit margins
Communication	Security and integrity of communication channels. For example, in military operations, communication is crucial for a warfighting organization to maintain synchronization. Just like the military, suppliers must have a reliable communication network. Natural disasters such as hurricanes can wipe out communication networks and stop a supply chain dead in its tracks.	Communication methods, Data protection, Involvement in innovation
Connectivity	To not be confused with connectivity of communications. In this context, it is the degree of interdependence and reliance on outside entities. For example, what is the scale and extent of the supply network? How often are services or products outsourced? The farther down the supply chain you go, the less control you have.	Reliance on information flow, frequency of outsourcing, Scale of network
Resources	Limits on productivity based on material requirements. During the initial stages of the COVID-19 epidemic, the sourcing of materials became increasingly difficult. Materials required for virus tests were unavailable and impeded production.	Natural resources, Raw material sources, effectiveness in sourcing

Now that you have an idea of what risks to look for while doing a risk assessment of your supply chain and suppliers, use the checklist downloadable on my site at https://hknapp.com/.

The check list encompasses all considerations discussed in the chart above. The check list provides a specific area average risk rating, weighted rating per area, and total overall rating. This checklist allows for you to rate a supplier while applying simple numbers and math to give you less of a skewed and subjective decision. The risk assessment uses a weighted average approach where the user inputs the importance of a specific factor from 1 being of low importance, and 5 being of high importance. When your total is added up, the importance of each rating is considered. The higher the number, the more desirable traits that specific supplier possess.

It can be used by your organization to better understand the risks in the supply chain and as a model to follow to get consistent results, no matter who conducts the assessment. Risks within your supply chain are constantly changing, so do these assessments regularly and update the chart when anticipating a risk event, such as a natural disaster.

CHAPTER 3:

Vendor Rationalization

Focus on resilience!

At this point, you should now have valuable information regarding your supply chain. You may have even identified a few suppliers you can grow with or noted others that are redundant, costly or just downright underperforming. This process of adding and removing suppliers is known as **vendor rationalization**.

Through the lens of resilience, having too many or not enough vendors can leave you prone to a disruption during an emergency.

That is why it is important to have a balanced number of suppliers in your supply base.

But what is the optimal balanced number of suppliers for your supply chain?

Vendor rationalization Concept:

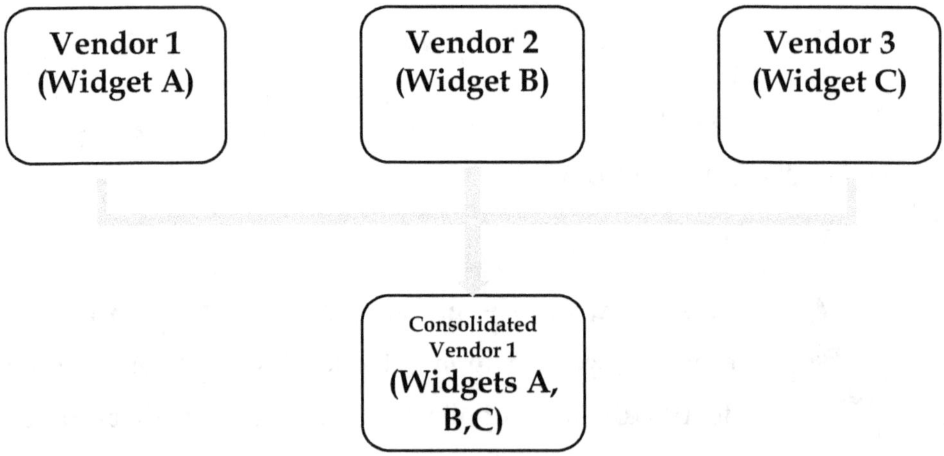

| Vendor 1 (Widget A) | Vendor 2 (Widget B) | Vendor 3 (Widget C) |

Consolidated Vendor 1 (Widgets A, B,C)

To answer that question, let's review the three main goals supply base rationalization:

Streamline the Organization's Spend

With a reduced number of suppliers to choose from, the procurement process can be simplified and more efficient. Having a limited supply base will allow you to focus your energy and time on suppliers that will make a difference. Communication channels can be improved, processes can be synchronized to benefit both organizations, and a relationship built on trust and respect can begin developing. This level of intimacy is difficult with a large supply base.

But there can also be a negative side to having a smaller supply base. Less supplier options can leave you dependent and without opportunities for procuring much needed materials or services, especially during a disaster. Determining the optimal number of suppliers is no easy task as there is no one-size-fits-all rule.

Depending on the company and products being sourced, many businesses like to have at least three suppliers per part or commodity. For example, one supplier may be awarded 80% of the company's business for the component, the second 15%, and the third 5%. By having three suppliers, the risk is distributed enough so that, in the case of an emergency, there will still be options available, and you'll have enough influence with your alternate supplier to make things happen.

Focused Buying Power for Purchasing Leverage

By purchasing more from a smaller number of suppliers, you can increase the level of influence within your supply chain. Some suppliers prioritize their workload by how much is being spent. When you are spending more, you improve your leverage on influence with the supplier and can possibly increase the chances that your work will be prioritized over others. Keep in mind, there needs to be a balance between competition and buying power. Pricing can become an issue since there the leverage of going to another supplier will be lost along with the ability to compare pricing and lead times.

Product Standardization

This approach aims to replace several products with a single product that has similar functionalities. This accentuates simplicity throughout the supply chain and manufacturing process.

Car manufacturers are great examples of how product standardization is done effectively. A side mirror used on a Toyota Corolla is also found on Camrys, Prius and even 4Runner SUV models. This allows the supply chain to have only one primary supplier for the mirrors, not one for each model, which would only complicate the supply chain leaving room for error.

With your goals and objectives in mind, here are some important factors to examine prior to the addition and removal of any supplier:

1. **Quantity and Dollar Value of Past Purchases from a Supplier** - Compare both the volume and dollar value spent with each supplier. Is there another supplier within your supply base that you can increase buying power with? If you spend more with a supplier, you build leverage. Not only from a money standpoint, but from a relationship standpoint as well.

2. **Number of Products Assigned to a Supplier** - Review the product or service distribution of that supplier. If only a few products are ordered, can another supplier that you already use satisfy those requirements?

3. **Any One-Time Suppliers** - In unique situations, a specific supplier will need to be used. If the supplier has not been

used in the last 2 years, the supplier can be removed from your list of active suppliers.

4. **Supplier Quality Records** - The quality of the product provided is one of the most critical factors to be considered during the vendor rationalization process. If a supplier does not deliver to the quality your organization requires, this should be an easy decision to remove that supplier.

5. **Supplier Performance** - Just like the track record of a supplier's quality is vital, so is the percentage of deliveries that are on-time or late. Late deliveries can have a negative impact on not only customer relationships but also on the operations of the entire business.

6. **Price** - There is a strong tendency for people to consider this the most important factor. Though it is important, price cannot be your only indication of value. Choosing a supplier simply based off a lower price may impact the delivery and quality of your product. You get what you pay for!

7. **Financial Stability** - Being involved with a supplier that is unable to meet financial obligations can lead to issues for your supply chain. A poorly managed supplier can default on product deliveries and can translate into a loss of financial investments made. Use the financial risk tools mentioned in chapter 1 to evaluate the financial stability of

a potential or current supplier. If an existing supplier is in financial trouble, you could help out your supplier out by paying a portion of upfront costs and agreeing to reasonable payment terms, such as NET 30 which means after 30 days of the invoice date, the invoice will be paid. For companies that have tight profit margins or low cash flow, getting the money from their sales sooner.

8. **Production Facilities and Capacity** - Analyzing the capacity of a supplier needs to be done with the awarding of each purchase order. Suppliers that are overutilized deliver products late or with poor quality. As I've personally experienced many times, a supplier will take on work knowing that they do not have the capacity to deliver on time. If possible, conduct an onsite analysis of your supplier to get an even better idea. It is recommended that suppliers have 10-15% of their capacity dedicated to emergencies.

9. **Compliance to Environmental Regulations and Policies** - Ensure that the supplier is compliant with all local, state, and federal regulations. Though it may not directly be your organization's fault, any unlawful actions can have an impact on the reputation of your business and/or monetary implications.

10. **Geographic Location** - Consider the needs of your supply chain. Do you need your suppliers to be geographically closer for control? Or is it better to have supplier dispersed

geographically so that a disruption event doesn't impact your entire supply chain? The notion of keeping suppliers as close to your organization as possible may not necessarily be what's best for your supply chain when building resilience.

With all of the disruptions, this specific topic has become the center of discussion for many companies. In response to the US and China trade wars and container shortages, many companies are moving out of China and moving either back to the United States, or to other countries such as India and Mexico to increase the ability to introduce products faster, respond to market changes, and minimize logistical risk.

Here are some of my personal favorite best practices:

- Have an evaluation system so that you can reward your important suppliers with long-term contracts. Long-term contracts will increase resilience by gaining long-term commitment from the supplier and lock-in pricing.

- Receive inputs and encourage participation of other departments.

- When moving from a larger volume of suppliers to fewer suppliers, ensure that the selected suppliers have the capacity and capability to support larger volumes while meeting your requirements in terms of quality and lead time.

- Don't reduce your supply base without establishing contractual relationships with new suppliers, otherwise risk disrupting the supply of products. Before you burn one bridge, make sure the other is built.

- Don't make price be the primary evaluation criteria. There are other factors to consider beyond the price. Instead, use price as only one piece of your entire criteria. Things like the quality of the product received and the on-time delivery (OTD) of the product are also very important for creating a resilient and efficient supply chain.

If you're finding this to be difficult to navigate or if you'd like extra support, I am available for personal consulting to discuss any issues.

CHAPTER 4:

Create a Business
Continuity Plan

With your analysis complete, the next step of a resilient transformation can begin. With so many disruptions in in the world, having timely and accurate information is not enough. You must be able to **sense and respond** to those changes. A strategy must be in place to re-plan and recalibrate during those changes. Gone are the days of relying on past performance and seasonal behaviors for accurate forecasts. The process I discuss next focuses on understanding your supply chain's vulnerabilities and identifying what actions to take to improve your supply chain's resilience.

Developing a strategic understanding of your current supply chain will now be helpful when you periodically engage with your stakeholders like vendors and other departments within your company.

Follow this process created by the US Department of Homeland Security and followed by the agencies such as the Department of Defense, to keep your supply chain running and profits flowing, especially during an emergency.

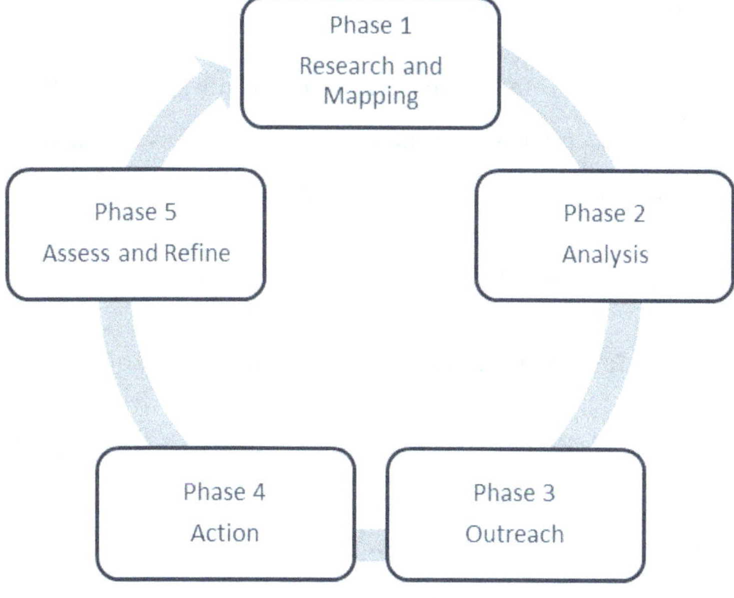

Phase 1: Research and Mapping

This phase utilizes data and details obtained from your supply chain analysis to identify and map out the structure of your supply chain. As we have seen during COVID-19, businesses must know where materials and suppliers are located. When issues arise, you need to be able to identify the source quickly and act immediately. Knowing these details will help you to not only create a plan, but also to create a plan that works. Follow these steps to research and map your supply chain:

1. Map out your entire supply chain to see the process flow from raw material to the end customer, so you can see your supply chain and identify choke points.

2. Identify primary suppliers and supply chain nodes (all the stops a product makes in the supply chain such as distributors, manufacturers, transportation hubs)

3. Prioritize the importance of your suppliers.

4. Include your findings from your infrastructure research.

Especially for resilience, having clear visibility of your supply chain past your tier 1 supply is a must. Tracing products down to your tier 2,3,4…. will give you even greater visibility. With your newfound visibility, do 2 things:

- Define what visibility means to your business

- Set specific goals on how your organization is going to leverage that visibility. What will you do with the information and how will you respond?

Here is a sample diagram of a simple supply chain:

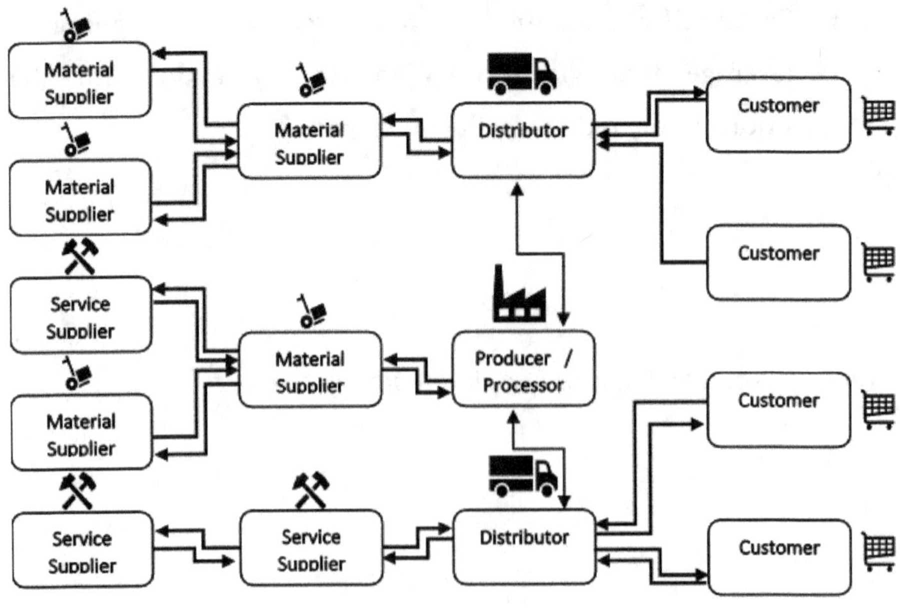

Material Supplier
Material Supplier
Service Supplier
Material Supplier
Service Supplier
Material Supplier
Material Supplier
Service Supplier
Distributor
Producer / Processor
Distributor
Customer
Customer
Customer
Customer

As you can see from the diagram above, a supply chain has the potential to span multiple countries, continents, specialties and even industries. Product and services can flow not just one way in a supply chain, things being returned or reworked.

To demonstrate, let us look at something simple, like a screw. A screw starts off as raw material like stainless steel, brass, or titanium. Once the raw material is sized and cut, it goes to a machine shop to be transformed into the actual screw shape. Depending on the specifications, the screw can be then sent for further processing such as heat treat, coating, or anodizing. From this basic example, you can see how a screw can move through multiple processes. These processes can be easily impacted by any type of disruption in your supply chain.

Phase 2: Analysis

Use this phase to tie together the findings from the first phase with your original weaknesses and abilities analysis from the second phase. Figure out the critical piece to keeping your supply chain resilient and asses their current capabilities.

Pinpoint the vendors within your supply base you may want to coordinate and synchronize your plans with, as they will become your key stakeholders.

In this phase, pause and ask yourself these questions:

1. What is the volume and velocity of my product flow on normal days?

2. What is the regular throughput?

3. How quickly can volume increase and be distributed?

4. Are my sources of supply dependent on critical infrastructure or other key resources?

5. What supplier do I contact if my primary supplier has been impacted?

Phase 3: Outreach

In Phases 1 and 2, you began the creation of a resilience plan with collected data. In the third phase, we use targeted meetings to validate your findings with stakeholders.

Phase 3 focuses on discussions with key stakeholders that review current priorities while identifying issues that must be addressed, so you gain alternate viewpoints and insights into areas that may have been missed.

Consider these best practices when initiating and holding discussions with supply chain stakeholders:

1) When opening a new relationship, visit the other party's place of business for a one-on-one informal discussion to build rapport and trust, which is critical to the success of your effort.

2) Consider asking for a tour of their facilities. This is often a good starting point, as the organization may enjoy showing off their facility, and it provides you with the opportunity to naturally ask occurring questions about how they operate, which will often serve to confirm or deny aspects of your Phase 2 analysis.

3) A discussion that cultivates trust is more likely to emerge from asking questions than from making statements. The same sort of questions asked in the prior analysis phase can be a good place to start.

4) Explain your concept for catastrophe preparedness and outline the desired end state. Emphasize the importance of their organization to the overall effort of maintaining resilience.

Phase 4: Action

The fourth phase is predominantly concerned with utilizing tabletop exercises. Think of tabletop exercises as rehearsals with your key stakeholders to review the collaborated resilience plan step-by-step.

A tabletop exercise is an activity in which key personnel are assigned roles and responsibilities and then meet to discuss, in a non-threatening environment, various simulated emergency situations. This may mean sitting down with all key stakeholders and drawing out your entire supply chain, like you did in phase 1, and reviewing how each specific emergency will impact the supply chain.

Using the COVID-19 outbreak example, one scenario for the exercise would be to discuss what actions need to be taken if there is an outbreak at one of your supplier's facilities. Who are your secondary suppliers that can be counted on to keep your product moving? How does this impact lead time? Who needs to be contacted? What will your main supplier do during the emergency to get back up and running as soon as possible?

Another new technique world-class organizations are using to maximize the efficiency and reliability of their supply chains involves analyzing data using cloud software. Companies such as Coupa, sell software that combines artificial intelligence with data analysis. With software like these, companies can plug in data from their MRP/ER/Spreadsheets along with specific scenarios to see what the potential impacts will be to the supply chain. Companies then can create specific scenario-based games plans that are tweaked for optimal effectiveness based on software predictions. This provides an entirely new level of insight for tabletop exercises and simulation planning which considers previous, current, and future data. Here is Coupa's website link if you're interested in learning more:

https://www.coupa.com/

Remember, a developed plan may look great on paper, but going through the motions step by step confirms understanding between all parties and may identify potential issues and inconsistencies. Supply chains are dependent not just on one person, but on synchronized operations.

Phase 5: Assess and Refine

This phase tends to be easily forgotten. As supply chains are constantly evolving, it is key to constantly review and refine the data, conduct additional analysis, and adjust your plans according to the information gathered. Maintain your efforts by refreshing collected data and revising the analysis at least once per year.

Another import piece of Phase 5 is maintaining the relationships that you have fostered and built. All the effort put into the previous four phases of this approach will be wasted without personal relationships. **A thoroughly thought out and financed plan will not work to its greatest potential if you do not have a solid relationship with your suppliers.** Remember, whether a vendor or a customer, a relationship cultivated and founded on trust and respect will always yield better results than a distant or poor relationship, especially during an emergency.

CHAPTER 5:

How to Use Business Continuity Plans

With a business continuity plan built for supply chain resilience, let's consider how to make the most use from your plans:

1. SENSE AND RESPOND TO CHANGING MARKET CONDITIONS – Especially with the events of 2020 and 2021, we all know that it is not enough to indicate that a disruption has or will occur, you must have a strategy in place to replan and recalibrate considering those changes. This guide will help

you develop that detailed plan which allow you to respond faster than the competition, ultimately giving you a competitive advantage.

2. CREATE AN EMERGENCY BUDGET – Having capital designated for those "just in case" moments are vital lifelines for a business trying to survive a crisis. For instance, companies that did not have funds dedicated to emergencies when the Coronavirus started to spread, unfortunately, could not pay rent, salaries, or cover operational costs. The most effective way to create flexibility for your organization and your supply chain is to have an appropriate emergency fund. You can withdraw from it to fulfill any financial obligation requirements you may have.

The steps below provide a framework for creating your emergency budget:

- Identify core expenses: Look through your regular business expenses and identify your most vital costs. It may also help to categorize each expense as a primary, secondary, and non-essential expense.

- Cash Flow Management: Make sure your receivables from customers are short and invoices promptly paid. By managing a healthier cash flow, unexpected expenses can be covered. You can also use your receivables to take out more cost effective loans if required.

- Consider opening a dedicated emergency account: Opening an account specifically for emergencies eliminates the risk of your emergency monies getting mixed in with other funds. It will also help monitor the rate at which your emergency fund is growing when you have enough funds.

3. REEVALUATE SAFETY STOCK LEVEL – Reassessing risk can also take the form of updating safety stock levels. Safety stock is a level of extra stock that is maintained exclusively to mitigate the risk of stock-outs. Sufficient safety stock levels allow businesses to have buffer stock if sales are aggressive or the supplier cannot deliver units at the expected time. Having too much safety stock can result in increased holding costs and risk that this cash is tied up in slow-moving and eventually obsolete products. Too little inventory can result in lost sales that lead to a higher rate of customer turnover.

It is also to understand that inventory does not necessarily have to take the form of tangible goods. Buffer inventory can take the form of surge capacity. This allows for a supply chain or business opportunity to ramp up production or distribution. Remember, capacity is not only the ability to produce product, but also the ability to store and move goods to market.

The most common factors taken into consideration when choosing a safety stock is:

- Demand: Analyze the number of items consumed by customers within a certain time frame.

- Lead Time: Determine the time it takes to receive an order after a customer places the order.

- Service Level: Calculate the probability of meeting demand with the current lead time and not stocking out.

If you wish to dig further into this topic: I found this article in Wikipedia to be helpful in explaining the safety stock calculations:

https://en.wikipedia.org/wiki/Safety_stock

4. THOROUGH CONTRACTING –The standard way that companies communicate contractual obligations is with a purchase order (PO). A purchase order is a document sent from a purchaser to a vendor to confirm a specific purchase of goods or services. Purchase orders by the buyer discuss what the order should contain and when it should arrive. It also includes details such as the items, quantity of those times, detailed descriptions, pricing at date of purchase, and payment terms.

Another significant component of a purchase order that helps with risk mitigation is the terms and conditions. Terms and conditions for purchase orders represent a legal contract between your company and the vendor. However, it can only protect your interests if you follow the legal requirements outlined in the terms and conditions.

Inaccurate or incomplete purchase orders can result in increased delivery times, incorrect product shipments, and even income loss due to returns and rework. In addition to the wrong POs, specific clauses in the purchase order should cover what actions to take during an emergency. These actions are priorities for existing and future orders or details of the cost escalation if the supplier fails to deliver.

Having clear and concise communication with organizations is pivotal for a successful supply chain.

5. IDENTIFY BACKUP SUPPLIERS AND SOURCES OF SUPPLY – It is critical to identify alternate suppliers that can provide the required services if your primary supplier(s) cannot deliver.

- Identify suppliers in alternate geographic locations, you can prevent one specific event from causing mass disruption to your supply chain.

- Classify and maintain a backup supplier for critical components within your approved supplier list. After that, your supply chain can continue its activities even on a temporary basis if for any reason your primary supplier is on hold.

- If you are scrambling to identify new suppliers during an emergency, you're too late.

6. REDUCE THE CONCENTRATION OF SUPPLY – This technique is unlike rationalizing the supply base that reduces the number of suppliers used from your approved suppliers' list. This method is used to mitigate the risk of disruption by reducing the dependence on a single supply line. Being overly reliant upon a constant and uninterrupted supply from a single point of origin like a vendor, country, or region is extremely risky. One regional catastrophe has the potential to seize up your entire supply chain operations and crash your business operations.

7. CYCLICAL REVIEW OF EMERGENCY PLAN WITH KEY STAKEHOLDERS – Having an emergency plan alone cannot mitigate logistical risks. You will need to review those plans annually with all impacted main stakeholders, at the minimum. The **suggested review frequency of your emergency plan with your key stakeholders is annual.** Our environment is evolving, so reviewing your plans frequently encourages collaboration within the supply chain. It also confirms a thorough understanding of the contents of your emergency plan.

(On my website, I also have a free e-book that covers this topic in detail.)

8. HIRE OR CONSULT WITH LOGISTICS EXPERTS - Companies such as 3rd, 4th, and even 5th party logistics providers are experts in logistical movements (for more info see appendix 2). You can contact them to assist with your desired level of logistical needs. (To learn more about outsourcing work to logistical experts, refer to appendix 2)

Next Steps:

Resilience Transformation

You now have knowledge and tools to thoroughly analyze your supply chain for all types of risk that can impact your supply chain and specific steps you can follow to reduce the impact of supply chain disruptions affecting you.

Here is a recap of the topics discussed:

Chapter 1: Supply Chain Analysis

Follow the PMESII-PT format to conduct strategic analysis of your supply chain.

Chapter 2: Risk Analysis

When analyzing your supply base, focus on the strengths and weaknesses of that supplier.

Chapter 3: Vendor Rationalization

Once you have an idea of which suppliers are worth continuing business with and which ones you wish to exit from, use vendor rationalization to have a concentrated and resilient supply base.

Chapter 4: Create Business Continuity Plan

When creating your plan, follow the five-phase cyclical approach. This plan focuses on not only creation, but also on maintaining and continually updating that plan.

Chapter 5: How to Use Business Continuity Plans

With a business continuity plan built for supply chain resilience, put the plan into action with specific actions on how to make the most of your plans.

Final Thoughts

This book covers the relationship between supply chain risks and business continuity. If you wish to learn more about the civilian and military principles, supply chain business continuity, resilience, emergency preparedness, emergency, and disaster management, click here:

https://hknapp.com/

Don't forget! If you need extra support or if you don't have the time but desire to do it yourself, I am also available by email for a one-on-one consultation or please email me at

howardsknapp@gmail.com with any of your questions.

I hope this guide helps you in creating a resilient supply chain that you know will operate no matter what is thrown at it.

While I would hope that this is not a farewell note to those of you who have found this information useful, but more importantly, and preferably, more of a welcome note.

<u>If you're new to Supply Chain:</u>

I would like to take this opportunity to welcome you to the start of a new future in your professional career as a supply chain manager in the supply management industry. You should be commended for seeking to better your professional opportunities for the future. You are taking the first step toward a bigger goal in life, and I wish to congratulate you.

Learning and understanding supply chain resiliency is taking the first step.

<u>To those Supply Chain veterans continuing your learning:</u>

I would like to take this opportunity to thank you for your continued efforts and professional development in your career as a Supply Chain Professional.

We can never learn too much & shouldn't stop learning.

To all of those who found this helpful – don't hesitate to contact me to review your supply chain and enhance its resiliency!

Visit…

https://www.linkedin.com/in/howardknappcpsm/

Appendix 1 –

Review of Logistics

The Oxford Dictionary defines logistics as the detailed coordination of a complex operation involving *multiple persons, facilities, or supplies*. Essentially, logistics is the planning, implementation, and control of efficient freight transportation and storage procedures from origin to consumption. Simply put, <u>logistics is any action that contributes to obtaining products or services from the supplier to the consumer.</u>

Primary functions of logistics.

<u>Logistics has seven primary functions. An organization must properly apply effectiveness and efficiency to each function of logistics to maintain the supply chain.</u>

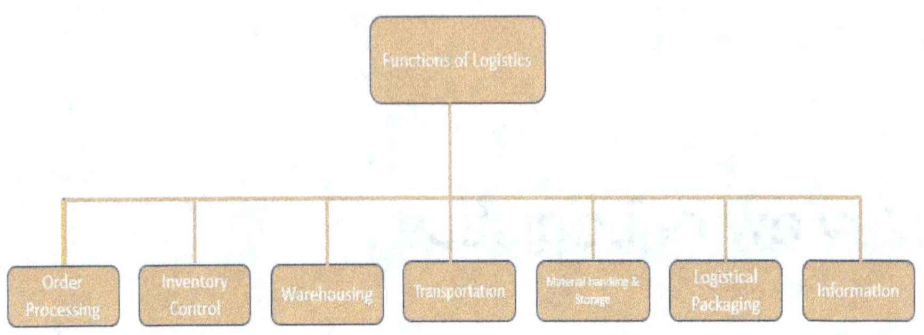

Order Processing

From a logistical perspective, order processing pertains to the <u>process of creating and issuing a purchase order (PO)</u>. The purchase order issued by a buyer or a designated representative shall specify the required appearance and performance specifications. The PO is a crucial legal document that contains the specific transaction between two parties, such as the instructions and expectations of the agreement. From the start of the process, perform this step correctly because inaccuracies create a negative domino effect on subsequent procedures. These inaccuracies could be manufacturing errors or delays in shipping products. Any detail that is unclear or inaccurate may be misinterpreted not only by the suppliers. One small mistake can compound and grow as misinformation travels down the supply chain.

Inventory Control

The process of managing stock once it arrives at a warehouse, store, or other storage location is known as inventory control. Inventory control aims to **balance the optimum level of inventory while maintaining an accurate inventory count.**

When it comes to "balancing" inventory, having too little stock can lead to stock-outs, lost sales, and even a loss of customers who go somewhere else for their needs. On the other hand, having too much inventory can lead to tied-up capital in excess inventory and an increase in overhead costs to maintain that inventory. The appropriate level of stock depends on the organization, the industry, and the nature of the business. However, some crucial factors are frequency of product sales, required safety stock level, cost of the product, size and dimensions of the product, and storage requirements.

From a military logistics perspective, stock-outs can be life-threatening.

Warehousing

The act of warehousing consists of storing and maintaining the product in the warehouse. Due to high product movement, the warehouse's dynamic environment presents unique risks. This risk is in the form of a product being lost, damaged, or stolen while in the warehouse. To minimize these dangers, a warehouse needs to have a clearly defined process for storing and picking products along with a neat and organized warehouse. I have learned that the act of keeping a store neat and tidy, while working in several warehouses, has been the single highest threat factor to risk mitigation. This detailing affects the most important aspect of a warehouse, inventory accuracy. Inaccurate inventory levels can lead to problems with other parts of the process, such as false promises to customers or purchasing having to expedite product delivery to meet commitments.

Material Handling and Storage

Material handling and storage involves moving goods to transfer points in the supply chain. For example, issues can arise when they move material from the vehicle into the warehouse space. The primary responsibilities in cargo handling consist of unloading, transporting, picking, and sorting. Poor cargo handling leads to financial loss and increased costs in product damage, product misplacement, and order delays. The frequent training of employees will improve productivity, quality, and safety.

Packaging

Many may not realize it, but there is a science to product packaging. Besides marketing, packaging protects the product, especially during transportation. The challenge of designing efficient packaging is to balance sufficient protection without incurring more costs than necessary, which comes with overprotection. Optimized packaging is an effective means of <u>reducing overall shipping costs</u> for any business, directly impacting the bottom line.

Information

Supply chains do not only move tangible items; they also move non-transferable items such as information. Relaying **accurate and timely information** is fundamental for procuring the right stuff, at the right place, at the right time, in the right quantity and right quality.

Logistics is an information-based activity of inventory movement across multiple organizations. As a buyer, I have communications with several of my suppliers daily. This connection is critical for supplier alignment. Issues and questions come up regularly. As a liaison, it is one of my primary functions to distribute information to the appropriate person for resolution. Just like during military movement, communication is critical for a well-orchestrated mission. Communication provides direction and instructions and is crucial for a healthy operating supply chain. A supply chain that does not operate cohesively cannot work efficiently. Supply chains must function like musicians in a symphony, completely in unison.

Transportation

When it comes to maintaining supply chain continuity, shipping is one of the most critical components. Although we use logistics and transportation interchangeably, there is a notable difference. For business owners and supply chain professionals alike, understanding the transportation of materials and products is essential. In the competitive business world, the product's movement must have the lowest cost to gain a competitive advantage.

When products are in transit, the risks include physical damage, limited infrastructure capacity, regulation, variable fuel costs, and weather conditions. It makes transportation an inherently risky activity.

Appendix 2 –

3PL, 4PL, 5PL

The following is a brief explanation that will help you decide the level of service your organization may need to agree upon before signing a contract:

3PL= In this model, the organization maintains management oversight. It also outsources operations of transportation and logistics to an external entity. That entity may subcontract some tasks. Additional services, such as crating, boxing, and packaging, add value to the supply chain.

4PL= When using a 4PL, an external organization will manage the logistics activities and the execution across the supply chain. For instance, a manufacturer utilizes a 4PL provider to outsource its entire logistics operations. This outsourcing can free up the resources of an organization to do other value-added activities.

5PL = With a 5PL, organizations can gain efficiencies and increased value from the beginning to the end of the supply chain by utilizing technology. 5PL providers also supply innovative logistics solutions and develop an optimal supply chain.

Besides freeing up time and capacity, logistical providers also provide these advantages:

Cost – Logistics providers allow shippers to gain access to a wide range of cost-saving benefits. These benefits include special rate pricing from carriers and the use of state-of-the-art logistics software that would not typically be available to the average vendor.

Stability – With rising instability in supply chains, providers can help reestablish balance. It is crucial to leverage their existing relationships with suppliers to ensure the supply chain continues to operate.

Capacity – With trucking capacity being limited, a carrier can help find available dimensions across one or more modes. They will use their robust network and economies to scale.

Visibility– Having detailed insight into your shipments has never been more critical in minimizing supply chain risk. The use of technology from logistics carriers identifies the problems early. It allows for preventative measures and solutions. This intervention prevents difficulties from becoming severe.

Additionally, be mindful of the risks associated with utilizing an outside logistic expert.

One of the key disadvantages of using a 3PL source is that it results in some loss of control over your shipping functions. When a business decides to join forces with a logistics provider, they trust the organization will adhere to the agreed upon terms and conditions. It may seem cheaper upfront to use a carrier, but it will likely be more expensive than handling the shipping function in-house. Turning these functions over to an external carrier is a primary commitment since your logistical team may lose much of the relevant market knowledge if the carrier is no longer in use. Thoroughly review the cost and benefits of using and not using a third-party logistics carrier.